DATE DUE

Animal Opposites

Fast

and

Slow

An Animal Opposites Book

by Lisa Bullard

consulting editor: Gail Saunders-Smith, PhD

content consultant: Zoological Society of San Diego

Capstone *press*

Mankato, Minnesota

Some animals move as fast as race cars.
Others are so slow they hardly move at all.
Let's learn about fast and slow
by looking at animals around the world.

Fast

Falcons are the world's fastest birds. They zoom through the sky in search of food.

Slow

Snails move very, very slowly.
They lug their shells
from place to place.

Fast

Cheetahs are the fastest animals on land. With quick bursts of speed, they chase down food.

Slow

Three-toed sloths move slowly through forest trees.

Sloths hang from tree branches almost all day. They even sleep while hanging upside down.

Fast

Sailfish dart through the ocean.
They are the world's fastest fish.

Slow

Seahorses aren't really horses.
They are very slow fish.

Fast

Fast zebras belong to the horse family.
They gallop away from danger.

Slow

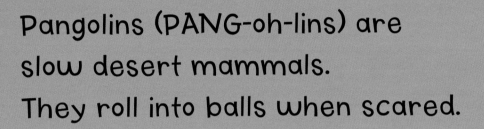

Pangolins (PANG-oh-lins) are
slow desert mammals.
They roll into balls when scared.

Fast

Dragonflies are fast-flying insects. They can quickly turn and zoom backward.

Some people call dragonflies mosquito hawks. Adult dragonflies eat hundreds of mosquitoes every day.

Bumblebees buzz slowly from flower to flower.

Fast

Ostriches can't fly.
But they run
faster than a horse.

Slow

Penguins can't fly either.
They waddle slowly
on their short legs.

Fast

Kangaroos take
big hops to travel fast.

Kangaroos and koalas are
marsupials. Female marsupials
carry their young inside
pouches on their bellies.

Koalas climb slowly through Australia's trees.

Fast

Pronghorns are the fastest
land animals in North America.

Slow

Slow-walking Gila monsters live in North American deserts.

Gila monsters are one of only two kinds of venomous lizards.

Fast

Orcas are also called killer whales.
They swim fast to hunt for food.

Slow

Manatees are slow water mammals. These gentle giants munch on sea plants.

Fast

During the day, gibbons swing fast through the rain forest.

Slow

At night, lorises slowly creep from branch to branch.

Fast

Hares hop fast to escape other animals.

Slow

Tortoises slowly carry
their shells along.

Tortoises can live
more than 150 years.

Some fast animals chase after food.
Others quickly run from danger.
Some slow animals climb through trees.
Others crawl across the ground.

What kinds of
fast and slow animals
live near you?

How Fast?

Bumblebees buzz along at about 5 miles an hour. People usually walk that fast.

Tortoises stroll from place to place at less than 1 mile an hour.

Snails move so slowly, they would take more than a day to travel 1 mile.

Falcons dive through the sky at 120 miles an hour.

Cheetahs sprint up to 70 miles an hour.

At a top speed of 40 miles an hour, kangaroos cover more than 30 feet in a single hop.

Reaching speeds of 30 miles an hour, dragonflies are one of the world's fastest insects.

Glossary

gallop (GAL-uhp)—to run fast

insect (IN-sekt)—a small animal with a hard outer shell, six legs, three body sections, and two antennas; most insects have wings.

mammal (MAM-uhl)—a warm-blooded animal that has a backbone and feeds milk to its young; mammals also have hair and give live birth to their young.

marsupial (mar-SOO-pee-uhl)—an animal that carries its young in a pouch

venomous (VEN-uh-muhss)—having or producing a poison called venom; Gila monsters have a venomous bite.

waddle (WAHD-uhl)—to walk with short steps while moving from side to side

Read More

Deegan, Kim. *My First Book of Opposites.* New York: Bloomsbury Children's Books, 2002.

Doinet, Mymi. *The Laziest.* Faces of Nature. New York: Random House, 2002.

Gordon, Sharon. *Fast Slow.* Just the Opposite. New York: Benchmark Books, 2004.

Hickman, Pamela. *Animals in Motion: How Animals Swim, Jump, Slither and Glide.* Toronto: Kids Can Press, 2000.

Internet Sites

FactHound offers a safe, fun way to find Internet sites related to this book. All of the sites on FactHound have been researched by our staff.

Here's how:

1. Visit *www.facthound.com*

2. Type in this special code **0736842748** for age-appropriate sites. Or enter a search word related to this book for a more general search.

3. Click on the **Fetch It** button.

FactHound will fetch the best sites for you!

Index

A+ Books are published by Capstone Press,
151 Good Counsel Drive, P.O. Box 669, Mankato, Minnesota 56002.
www.capstonepress.com

1 2 3 4 5 6 10 09 08 07 06 05

Library of Congress Cataloging-in-Publication Data
Bullard, Lisa.
    Fast and slow: an animal opposites book / by Lisa Bullard.
    p. cm.—(A+ books. Animal opposites)
    Includes bibliographical references (p. 31) and index.
    ISBN 0-7368-4274-8 (hardcover)
    1. Animals—Miscellanea—Juvenile literature. 2. Animal locomotion—Miscellanea—Juvenile
literature. I. Title. II. Series.
QL49.B7748 2006
590—dc22   2005000063

Summary: Brief text introduces the concepts of fast and slow, comparing some of the world's
        fastest animals with animals that are slow.

Credits
Donald Lemke, editor; Kia Adams, designer; Kelly Garvin, photo researcher;
    Scott Thoms, photo editor

Photo Credits
Ardea/Jean Paul Ferrero, 16; Ardea/M. Watson, 22; Brand X Pictures/Burke/Triolo, 1;
Brand X Pictures/John Lambert, 27 (zebras); Bruce Coleman Inc., 9; Bruce Coleman
Inc./Alan Blank, 19; Bruce Coleman Inc./Hans Reinhard, 7; Bruce Coleman Inc./Kim
Taylor, 13; Bruce Coleman Inc./Pat Hagan, 21; Bruce Coleman Inc./Tom Brakefield, 2;
Bruce Coleman Inc./Tui A. De Roy-Moore, 25; Corbis/John Conrad, 10; Digital Vision/
Gerry Ellis, 1 (tortoise and ostrich), 2 (koala), 26 (tortoise), 27 (ostrich); Digital Vision/
Gerry Ellis & Michael Durham, 26 (dragonfly); Digital Vision/Joel Simon, 1 (penguin),
(penguins), 15; Digital Vision/Stephen Frink, 3 (seahorse); Digital Vision Ltd., 3 (chee
Getty Images Inc./Andy Rouse, 6; Getty Images Inc./Frank Lane/Parfitt, cover; Getty
Images Inc./Mick Martin, 5; James P. Rowan, cover; Minden Pictures/Frans Lanting,
Minden Pictures/Mitsuaki Iwago, 14; Minden Pictures/Thomas Mangelsen, 4; Peter
Arnold, Inc./Dennis Nigel, 11; Peter Arnold, Inc./Gerard Lacz, 17; Photodisc/G.K. & V
Hart, 2 (bumblebee), 27 (snail); Seapics.com/Doug Perrine, 8; Tom & Pat Leeson, 18

Note to Parents, Teachers, and Librarians
This Animal Opposites book uses full-color photographs and a nonfiction format to
introduce children to the concepts of fast and slow. *Fast and Slow* is designed to
be read aloud to a pre-reader or to be read independently by an early reader.
Photographs help listeners and early readers understand the text and concepts
discussed. The book encourages further learning by including the following sections:
How Fast?, Glossary, Read More, Internet Sites, and Index. Early readers may need
assistance using these features.